Drawing on Life

Poems

Mason Drukman

Art
Lisa Esherick

Fomite
Burlington, VT

Copyright 2014 © by Mason Drukman
Art copyright © by Lisa Esherick

ISBN-13: 978-1-937677-69-5
Library of Congress Control Number: 2014936044

Fomite
58 Peru Street
Burlington, VT 05401
www.fomitepress.com

Cover Art - Lisa Esherick

For Sam
I miss you.

Contents

An American Family	1
An Eye for Taste	4
Dressed to Kill	6
Uncle Harry	7
I Know What You Mean, Ivan Karamazov	9
Bob	10
I'm Driving Dave Dellinger	12
The Lady	14
Snow Geese in the Berkeley Pit	16
Things Fall	18
One Eye for Survival	20
The Freelancer	21
The New Old Math	23
Political Theory (for Matt Stolz)	25
Incubation	27
Father, 1989	29
Red Car	31
Gin	33
Sally	36
Balance Rock	38
The Baseball Lesson	40
Who's Afraid in the Dark	42
Safe Havens	44
Come to Jamaica	45
She Could Have Been Right	47
Switchback	49
On the Sundial Bridge	50
Way After Sappho	51
Isidor Wright	52
Loma Prieta	53
Birth of the Blues	56
Shipping News	58
Weekend Pass	59
He Didn't Come	62

In my dream thoughts	64
Kidneys	65
The Watsu Water Massage	66
Norman Jacobson	67
Awakening	68
Ice	70
The Lobsterman	72
Seeing/Unseen	74
Why Didn't You Call?	75
P.S. Do You Read Me?	76
Anomie	77
Whose Woods	79
Rainy Day Rumblings	81
David Carlson's *Quantum Quartet*	82
ALL	84
Goodbye	86
. . . for Sore Eyes	88
Still Life	90
The Grief Group	92
A Conversation	94
Mechanical Disadvantage	95
Getting in Touch	97
Once My Moon	98
Note	100
Acknowledgements	101

An American Family

the white birch sits where it belongs
snugged within its shining family
on the shore of the Merrimack

a sister tree stands on the opposite coast
blazing whiteness against
the uncertain red of cold-snapped sequoias

the Billerica summer house
a mordant aroma of faded woodwork
emptied rooms in dead-leaf brown

the Miami daughter
who can no longer stand
sits in her wheelchair
under a beetling
waiting for help

her New England sister
leans out toward the parking lot
of her subsidized apartment
her Chevy wagon
buried in snow

the brother in Georgia
reclines on his sectional
both feet on the hassock
flipping the remote
trying to remember

the father who smoked
two packs a day
sometimes three
windows closed tight
in his cobalt De Soto

baby brother
younger than he used to be
dials long distance
no message left
and no one rings up in return

mama's gone missing
she stands in the woods
by a dying birch
unable to see
through cross-hatched glasses

the eldest son
refuses to be in this poem
an undomesticated redwood
blockades his back yard
obstructing our view of his life

An Eye for Taste

like a platypus under water
he eats with eyes shut
the better to focus on the essence of the fare
every crumb of Panko
every shred of saffron
every molecule of rose water
and after dessert
dilates on what he's ingested
takes pleasure in listing the ingredients
in seldom missing one or
mistaking one for another

his eyes are also closed when he sings
an Irish tenor with red hair wearing dark glasses
at a Sears Roebuck upright
crooning not the cèilidh melodies
or step-dance ditties of the Old Sod
but the ballads of McCartney and Lightfoot and
medleys of folk tunes and klezmer laments

in the ICU his eyes never close
as far as anyone can see
alone of the nurses
he wears shades indoors
against regulations
the only male on the shift
a giant among women
his large body moving nimbly his voice
a humming accompaniment to the susurrations
of the medication pumps and breathing apparatus

his team is shocked when he's dismissed from his job
after half a day's duty in the operating room
where he's worked off and on many times in the past

outraged that the union does not file a grievance
mystified when he does not appeal or talk to a lawyer
saddened when he leaves the building and never comes back

after he has been declared legally blind
he mentions (over an Indian meal
prepared by his daughter featuring
chicken with coriander tamarind and asafetida
each of which he identifies with his very first bite)
how simple it can be for a man to miss certain things
when his field of vision narrows in the light

Dressed to Kill

listen to: lotusland dreamers, spectral romantics—
Death is:
sexy: a beguiling seducer with an amorous touch
mythic: a faceless apparition in a hooded cloak
benign: an I.V. drip, killing softly with lorazepam & morphine
that's a lady we can live with

no no—drop all delirium:
Death unfrocked inhuman sanguineous—
the bullet shatters the skull at the cerebral aqueduct
the spear rips through the nipple, severing the heart sack
the embolism hammers the sternum, turns the chest blue
a predator drone erases three toddlers in point seven seconds
no one can live with that woman

a show of hands on the main propositions—
       prop one: nobody's program is infinitely renewable
       prop two: we seldom get the ending we wish for
       prop three: Death is a bitch, however she's dressed
       prop four: killing A to save B is worthwhile and just

props one two and three are cautiously agreed to—
prop four has a problem—the realist's hesitation—
maneuver as we might, Death's no redeemer—
all hands are counted—four fails by a landslide

I voted for four

Uncle Harry

said boychick listen
we need a doctor in this family
I don't want you to grow up to become
you should excuse the expression
a shyster lawyer like your cousin Myron

Uncle Harry ran the Drake Theatrical Agency
a grand name that stirred the imagination
Toys in the Attic
A Month in the Country
Hellzapoppin

the USO appeared at my overseas base
with New Englanders on the bill
did they know my uncle?
you mean Harry Drake the booker?
hey, this guy's uncle is Harry Drake, the booker

Uncle Harry "handled acts"
jugglers, musicians, elephants, magicians
artistes he could place
in a lounge, in a tent, in the Shubert even
Broadway Danny Rose he was
from an office on Boylston

Uncle Harry married once,
Velma a mid-twenties tapper
from the chorus line in *Gypsy*
she left him after fourteen months

it's okay, boychick, it's okay
you're right, she's a shtunk
but I already knew that

the bouquet of Harry's rooms
Aqua Velva and Brylcreem
bleeds into the hallway of his apartment building
after the funeral his brothers find a 1919
application to a pre-med program at Tufts
on his desk in a stamped envelope
filled out in pencil
unsigned

I Know What You Mean, Ivan Karamazov
*it's just the angelic confidence of the child who has no refuge
and no appeal.*   Fyodor Dostoyevsky

I long wished the angel of death on my side
to finger the villains of my choosing
with such control I could have been a better person
happier stronger safer.

Hitler, for starters, his Nazi followers
and the rest of the fascists racists imperialists Stalinists
tyrannizing victims all over the world.

And especially our homebred actors of evil
the fulsome: Laird, Rusk, the brothers Bundy
the odious: Rice, Haldeman, Erlichman, North
the shameless: Weinberger, Powell, Rostow, Abrams
the execrable: Kissinger, McNamara, Reagan, Rove
the assassins: Nixon, Johnson, Bush
to name only the most deserving.

And of course my father—omnipotent oppressor—
peerless wielder of the unspared rod.

The beating continues
for a minute, for five minutes, for ten. . . .
The child screams. At last the child cannot scream, it gasps,
"Daddy, daddy!"

Bob

not counting computers or cell phones,
not counting wrist watches or appliances
my brother Bob keeps thirty-nine clocks in his house
he's a collector—of clocks

also of songs
tunes
melodies
lyrics
arrangements
renditions
solos
riffs
orchestrations
syncopations
all in his head

Ellington, Porter, Gershwin, Styne,
Cy Coleman, Dave Frishberg, Johnny Mercer
    I heard you call for an all-star band....
    When the deep purple falls....
    Boop boop dit-tem dat-tem what-tem Chu....

saxophone clarinet flute, Bob's played the Boston Sound
sideman and maestro—gig after gig—fifty-five years
the Boston Sound
a little Jimmy Dorsey a little Shep Fields
a lot of Guy Lombardo—minus the frou-frou
you know it as the music you
moved to at BMs and weddings
boogied to at Nuttings on the Charles

fingertips dibbity-dab the face of the dashboard
toes tap the tile under the kitchen table

    Blues in the Night
    Those Little White Lies

maintain the chops
take it from the top
riffs on the riffs keeping time

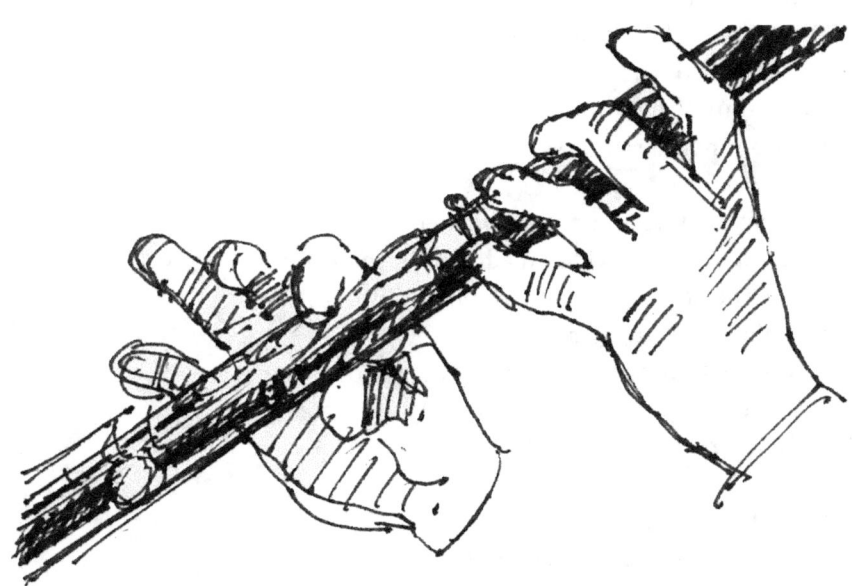

I'm Driving Dave Dellinger

to a meeting
he's in the back seat writing
a speech he will deliver in twenty minutes
as we cross the Willamette River
on the Burnside Bridge

in my powder-blue Ford sedan
that looks alabaster
in the evening glare of springtime

a loud grinding noise
then a thud
brings the '54 four-door
to a dead stop
in the center lane of a span
still crowded with
too-fast just-past-
rush-hour traffic

with my driveshaft on the pavement
I send Dave in a taxi to an address in the Albina
where the Society for New Action Politics (SNAP)
of which I am president
is waiting to hear his take on what is happening
elsewhere in the anti-war movement—
he'll be late but he'll get there

I won't
with my broken universal joint—
    (a contrivance providing
    a synchronic connection
    between two moving components of a driveshaft)
    descendent from the invention

in the third century BCE
by Philo of Byzantium
of the gimbal
whose improvement
dubbed *pithékon*
by Atheneus Mechanicus
two-hundred years later
allowed warships to yoke together
in coordinated siege against enemy cities—
now lying in pieces on the Burnside Bridge

The Lady
Then fled she to her inmost bower
            Alfred Tennyson

It's a regular meeting of the poetry group, we're
reading Japanese translations by Rexroth when a
long-haired big-breasted naked lady comes in, sits
herself down on my lap and asks is there anything she
can do for me. Of course I'm flustered and to buy a
little time I ask her name and she says Godiva but you
can call me God which is OK by me though I'd prefer
Goddess because that's what she looks like
with those *rippled ringlet*s and ruby-red nipples.
Meanwhile the six women in the group
all older than God
are looking you might say uncomfortable or even
daggers and the other three men are thinking holy
Christ or what happens next or is this someone he
knows and my lap is getting moist and I say in a hard-
to-hear voice that I can't at the moment think of
anything God could do and maybe we should just
continue our reading and I wonder aloud whether she
might have the wrong house and she couldn't be a
friend of my sister's could she? And she replies t'was
me who told her to come all *clothed in chastity* and
now we must go. Our horse is waiting and she must
re-clasp *the wedded eagle*s of her belt. And what the
hell I get up full of Godliness and with a look on my

face follow her out the door when through the other
door steps my wife who peers out the window
watching us trip down the path shrugs and (echoing
Saigýo) says:
Why should I be bitter
About someone who was
A complete stranger
Until a certain moment
In a day that has passed?

Snow Geese in the Berkeley Pit

In delta formations filling the sky
Canada snow geese pause in mid-flight
hovering over the Berkeley Pit
as if weighing inducements
  your journey is long
  come rest in our stillness
  come drink our refreshment.

Do they notice the strangeness
treeless, sienna, the smell of metallic
like no other stop on their migrating flyway?
not Old Wives Lake
not Isla El Fuerte
not the tarn atop Tamalpais.

A beguiling chorus from Butte's Great Divide
Our Lady of the Rockies
Madonna of the mountainside
  nothing to fear friends
  nothing to fear.

In cascading patterns they drop to the water
softly soft on the cupreous water
four hundred mouths immersed in the water
three hundred dead in the toxic first hour.

And what of the humans of Silver Bow County
on Iron Street on Platinum, West Gold and Galena
What shall we do with our lake of affliction?
Amplifiers hard by the Pit
ear-splitting dissonance hammering the wasteland
a warning to wild things to keep a safe distance
(plus a lookout and gift shop to accommodate tourists).

Things Fall

Left leg dangling from the edge of the roof
foot feeling for the wobbly stepladder
the Pacific shoreline cambers
blue-on-russet-on-gold on south to Nehalem—
Neahkahnie Mountain stares past the pitched roof
past the composite shingles & re-pointed chimney—
but it didn't have to be like this (exactly).

Contact is made between foot and ladder
the ladder shudders just out of reach
sunshine glistening off moist pine needles
trapped in the gutter along the eaves—
I wonder (I know) how I got into this mess.

The ladder teeters, dives towards the deck
followed hard by foot and torso
one might have arranged a later visit
(or none at all, if given the choice)
although she came six-thousand miles
although she *had* to see me (she said).

I might overshoot the deck entirely
land in the blackberry thorns, I might even be—
those letters, the ones I should have burned—
first threads of silver fog—
I must have promised certain things (I didn't)—
coiling among the treetops (or didn't mean to).

*Douglas firs grow taller
as the observer is descending*
she'll be here tomorrow
it's time to take action (what?)—
if I had it to do over, I'd be more careful—
I always pass [—] on good advice.

One Eye for Survival

My sister is seeing double
as I did long ago.
Diplopia: everything in twos.
It's a bird-bird.
It's a plane-plane.
Major Major-Major Major.

Advice to the brain: use but one eye at a time.
Alternating exotropia. Stereopsis out.
Ahab scanning for the whale.

My sister began seeing double
When her husband died.
He was a survivor.
Given six months he lasted six years.
Survival: death by another name.

My sister shed tears equally from both of her eyes.
Sitting shiva her three sons tell jokes
Check cell phones send out for pizza.
In the din they could be six.
She feels her husband shining.
With a single eye in focus
She alone can see to see his light.

The Freelancer

there's our writer now
in his red shirt
a drink in hand
floating across the room
a smile on his smile

and yowza he's got a paying job
a book about cancer
a feel-good guide aimed at survivors
a bigger market than you think
if you factor out pancreatic lung and liver

of course he knows nothing about the subject
but neither does the fat cat that hired him
who just lost his father to
a bladder tumor whose breakaway cells
moved fatally to dad's cerebellum

in his father's memory
the son wants to tell survivors—what?
how lucky they are?
how happy they should be?
how to get over it?

whatever the message
our author will deliver it
a freelancer in moth balls
he's glad to be writing something, anything
glad to be someone's ghost
if that's what it takes
will his name be on the cover?
that he can't tell you

he deletes a zero
from his logarithmic computation
leaving a hole through which he drops
into an ocean of blood cells

disfigured, pathological
but friendly, affectionate
pouring through his arteries
with effusions of love

a call from the doctor
waits on his smart phone
his labs show blood-count anomalies
the nurse has set up a sonogram

in his mail slot
an announcement from the publisher
Your deadline will not be extended.

The New Old Math

1
like angel dust from a dealer
his words had kept her calm
and quiet
now she felt her power

2
those profligate years
she wanted them back
the formula: art + 1 artist = happiness^2
whose formula was that

3
Smith girls sucked G & Ts through straws
supposing godlings with creased pants
and clear complexions

4
for her a love affair with Paris
breathing free from *le cinquième étage*
vin extraordinaire in unwashed mugs
compagnonnage behind canvas partitions
a continuous *hommage* to living in the arts

until the celebration stopped
at aversion—then loathing—
followed by violence

5
his addiction to Smirnoff
exceeded hers to the Louvre
nearly equaling her great urge to kill
she dreamt first of murder
his death and her freedom—and finally
(in *le Métro* back from the hospital)
of an altered equation

art *minus* one artist equals:
illusion's end
with no further sequels

Political Theory (for Matt Stolz)
Habituate yourself to walk very fast.
                            Thomas Jefferson

I'm rifling my mind
seeking a passage which
if it came to me
might make the difference.

The meeting is about to commence
(I'm just a little nervous) to consider
The Early Demise of Practical Action
and what (in the end) do we mean by the end.

(I'd like—if they'd let me—to slink away
for an interval of non-recognition
but the room's full of looks.)

The argument comes down to the usual—
take on our enemies or settle for safety
Side A: We must protect ourselves.
Side B: They are all out to get us.

Edmund Burke: *The concessions of the weak are the concessions of fear.* (True, but not what I was looking for.)

Bertold Brecht: *In a good country virtues wouldn't be necessary.* (Burke, again, when you think about it.)

Arnold Toynbee: *No annihilation without representation.*
(Good, very good, but slightly off-topic.)

Franz Kafka: *People under suspicion are better moving than at rest.*
(That's it.)

That's it exactly.

Brothers and sisters, I propose a rapid relo . . .

This just in: Drukman says proceedings were disrupted by a series of explosions causing untold . . .

Incubation

1
He came on line already wounded.

2
I am five
At the Beth Israel Hospital three men hold me down
a fourth places a padded cup over my nose and mouth.
They do it again when I am six. Again at seven.
I come to know I will not see Snow White or Bambi.

3
What do preemies learn in incubators?
Self-absorption? Self-deception? Self-government?
In-utero-post-partum-*Where's-Waldo?*
Later he remembered what he had tried to forget.

4
When I tell my father I trudge seven miles a day
as a caddy at the golf course, he doesn't believe me.
When I tell him the Japanese have bombed
Pearl Harbor, he doesn't believe me.
When they didn't tell me my mother was dying
I believed them.

5
You walk into a broadcast studio.
The announcer flips on the mike and
asks you if you think a certain company committed fraud.
Though you don't hear the question you say
"generally speaking that's an accurate observation."
The defamation suit runs to seven figures.

6
Not only did the reviewer misconstrue your meaning
fail to read the introduction
get the chronology wrong
she also misspelled your name.

7
I don't remember the day Kennedy died.
I was busy reading *Metamorphosis*.
(To tell you the truth, I do remember that day
but I am not what you would call a reliable witness.)

8
Untimely ripped.

9
They say there is no cure.

Father, 1989

Dad's here, again
flew out on Delta
changed planes at Denver
The meat was like leather

he's now 86 looking like 70
goes for sitcoms and thrillers
Ludlum and Lear
recalls the Red Sox announcer
from the early days in Boston
There was a shmuck

he reads the paper with his good eye
front page to back
Look at these prices
Home it's much cheaper
Goddam gonifs

the sisters-in-law at canasta
Esther: *She didn't have to settle for him*
Fanny: *She dated Walter Pidgeon*
Rosie: *She could have married the doctor*
Eva: *She went for the sex*

he besieges the toilet
abdominal salvos
enema bag streaming
conduit dripping
Where is that towel?
Sonofabitch

the old gentleman's leaving
flying back through Houston
One lousy meal
They can kish meer in tochas

Red Car

If you become upset while driving, you should
    a. control your emotions while continuing to drive
    b. park the car and "cool down"
    c. speed up, to reach your destination faster
    d. roll down your window and "cool off"
Traffic School Test Question

on one of those inclines northwest of Mt. Shasta
escape routes for big rigs with dubious hydraulics

five cars coeval ascend
the snaky approach from the south
to the crest where two lanes become three
a smooth straight shot to the valley

Black Beauty Imperial with Cato at the wheel
Arnold off-location in a gunmetal Hummer
an aging scribe steers a small red Toyota
Rita Moreno in a lavender limo
Andy Granatelli and his golden Avanti

stretto con tosto, tutti concertare

an automotive quintet in perfect synchronicity
like a five-linemen phalanx running interference
like a wedge of Blue Angels buzzing the stadium
like simultaneity before Einstein said no

we learn from snopes dot com
that state police never single out
red vehicles for road violations
how does snopes know this?
they asked the highway patrol

they didn't ask the cop hiding by the on ramp
outside Yreka on Interstate 5

Gin

he says, " J-I-N, gin."
His discard snaps face-down on the stack.
Despite its chestiness
she believes his "gin" is declared without venom.
He's not Hume Cronin.
This isn't *The Gin Game*.
She's not Jessica Tandy.
But she wonders, as it slices across the table,
isn't his pronouncement coated with attitude?

It's not just his ginning.
It's the twenty-seven points
he takes from her hand to win the game.
His second in a row.
Third out of four.
She shoots him a smile.

Still dripping from the salt water spa
they're relaxing over cards
after a day at Joshua Tree Park
and a hike through Hidden Valley
where they'd hoped, with no luck,
to catch a glimpse of native wildlife,
desert iguanas, coyotes or quail,
giving up when even a road runner
failed to appear, settling finally for
a pair of crows in an argument.

They'd been disappointed by the lack of fauna
and exhausted from climbing among
the boulders and rock configurations
rising like fortresses or monsters
every cluster a contributor to the collective persona:
eye sockets, noses, grimaces
grizzly paws, dragon heads, leviathans
a panoply of penises and vulvas
outsized buttocks like a meeting of moons.

"I'm knocking for four," she says.
He pauses. Puts down his cards.
Covers her four of hearts with two black deuces.
"I'm afraid, darlin', that's all I've got.
I believe that puts me out."

It's the "I believe" she can hear,
if she wants to, as patronizing:
he knows very well
the ten-point insult
will give him the game.

She'd rather not want to.
She dwells for a moment on his wet naked body.
They are not in a stage play.
She's known him since college.
Always respectful.
Always the sweet one.
Except in a card game.
Then he's Hume Cronin—
in spades.

Sally

Won't you come home, dear Sally
Come home to me, dear Sally
Did someone do you wrong?

everything changed when you
mastered the windows
but the truth is you had left
more than once in the past

during the war
for the army post on Henry's Hill
searching for enemy planes
on the South Shore of Boston

no bombs on the hill
detonations in your house
voices provocation the endless discord
is that why you vanished?

small for an Alsatian
the sharpness of the breed
waiting at every crossroad
sprinting ahead in my chosen direction

rusty withers on brown and chocolate
your smell of fresh hay in the wind
we swam together at Glen Echo Lake
I kissed you on the bridge of your nose

locked alone in the house
you pried up the handle
of a casement window
paw print scratches on a maplewood sash

what was it exactly?
not competition from
the black and white tabby
fighting for space
in front of the oil stove

not that you were kept in at times
the yard full of snarling males with red erections
(two litters in your lifetime
but you hated the sex)

though you never complained or got angry
you knew you had to escape:
from the family that loved you
with too much distraction

Balance Rock

to find your way back to Balance Rock
you start below the dry waterfall
at the east end of Wagner's Pond
try to follow the rabbit path along the rill
skirting the hotchpotch of skunk cabbage
purple and green and stinking

you pass a stand of pussy willows
a circle of lady slippers
dewy pink labia
sepals cupped like a young boy's balls

the trail vanishes
the ground rises
the woods thicken
sycamore and buckthorn
black birch and oak
at the one slippery elm
you wonder which way is next

the terrain grows rocky
a high-bush blueberry patch
its ladybug colony feeding on aphids
an anthill reaching three hands high
girding the trunk of a dying maple
you're almost there

Balance Rock never wavers
lit silver in the sun
spherical equipoised
twenty feet high thirty across
one toe on bedrock
rising from below

did you claw to the top
on the craggiest side, or was it a dream
did you lower a rope to hoist up Marie
or did she scale the same surface quicker than you

did she nibble your lip and cradle your cock
lord of the forest
King of the Rock

The Baseball Lesson

Dom DiMaggio (before Pearl Harbor, before I was ten).
Bespectacled, proficient. "The Little Professor"
Better fielder than brother Joe.
You don't think so?—you must be from New York.
Years later, I hand-packed two quarts of strawberry ice cream
for Dom at a snack shop in Humarock.
I never let on I knew who he was.

What's he mumbling now?

The '41 Red Sox. Fenway Park.
My uncle's box behind third.
I had their signatures, the whole team,
on a brand-new baseball.
Autographed. Official. Major League. *Mine.*
A lineup of all-stars. Super performers.
Five would make it to the Hall of Fame.

He goes on and on, doesn't he?

Joe Cronin, jut-jawed shortstop,
rough and tumble, clutch in the clutch.
Player-manager, married the boss's daughter.
Couldn't beat the Yankees, but who could?

He said something about his boss's daughter.

Jimmie Foxx, old "Double-X" ("one-xer"
Pete Fox was also on the team). Babe-like slugger,
"The Beast," 3-time MVP, triple-crown winner. Legs almost gone,
but still feared by pitchers & hitting .300 (not to mention Bobby
Doerr or Lefty Grove).

Let's roll him over so we can wash his backside.

And Ted Williams. Did you think I'd forgotten "The Kid."
"The Splendid Splinter," "Teddy Ballgame."
Sinuous motion. John Wayne looks.
Rodin's *Adam* with a bat in his hands.
We don't care that he never tipped his hat.
The purest hitter in baseball history.
Departed the game with a homer.

His blood pressure's running dangerously high.

I had the baseball, it was mine.
I should have held onto it, but the Simpson brothers
pressured me into using it in a pickup game
on the side of the hill behind their father's corn patch.
The seventh batter (not me) hit it over the stone wall
into a neighboring tangle of boxwood and briars.
Though we searched until sundown, we never could find it.

I wish now—when I need it—I still had that baseball.

Who's Afraid in the Dark

1
Arriving on schedule
Panic flies off for she knows
Though I slip from the precipice
I will float safe and unhurt
Through comforting mist into morning.

2
I share dreams with colleagues
Who seem to know mine in advance.
Fearful naked unready
Unable to locate lovers or friends.

3
Panic's returned
And fills me at the wheel of a '64 Valiant
Fishtailing backwards down a slippery incline.
Head spinning. Her voice screaming
No footbrake. No handbrake.

4
I fight through a midnight forest
Frightened/unfrightened by howls and confusions.
Alumnus of closet detentions
Sent home early. Tattered and wet.
Oak door slammed tight and locked.

5
In this house of stratagems I need you.
Your voice alone in every alcove.
A fiery glance singes my beard.
It's someone I know.
And I know it's not you.

Safe Havens

1
My father used to talk about his "men"—his skin man, his eye man, his ear-nose-and-throat man. His heart-and-lung man predicted he would die within months if he continued sucking nicotine into his obstipated chest. So he dropped his pack-a-day habit at age eighty-seven and—with inbred ill temper intensified by abstinence—extended his life another five years.

2
I found refuge from the torment of family
in a '33 Plymouth
derelict in the dirt at the end of the driveway
soothed by the smell of humidified mohair
palpitant drops on the oxidized roof
streaming like tears
down the cracks in the windshield.

3
Now I have my own array of men (and women)
urologist
nephrologist
endocrinologist
and I don't have the fortitude
as the end moves in closer
to tell these good people
they can all kiss my ass.

Come to Jamaica

Ocho Rios
twilight on the shore
ganja in the air
soirée al fresco
behind a chain-link fence

sloe-eyed Tranquility
modeling a wraparound
Caribbean special
four hundred American

limbo at the lowest
sand-sticky legs
strapless bikini
Adeline's the winner
(from North Carolina)

rental car in the hills
above Old Spanish Town
two-ton banana truck dead in a ditch
forty-three thin men
heaving it upright

fusillades of rocks
raining on the rental car
backing down the road
at sixty miles an hour

glistening Rasta
undulant crotch
Adeline's cleavage
and at the next table
rum-soaked Rosie
(from Mansfield Ohio)

do it to her do it to her
for chrissake go get her

a Montego specialist in the sweeping of sand
a voice from the lowering shadows
in Jamaica he says
everyone be gonna get fucked

She Could Have Been Right

He confronted it first, the ethos,
on his second day in New Zealand
caught on Queen Street in Auckland traffic
in a taxi maneuvered byWiremu
on his way to the airport late
for a flight to his new job in Wellington.
He asked if they couldn't go faster.
Wiremu, quietly,
Not to worry, mate. She'll be right.

She'll Be Right.
A social philosophy.
A cultural persuasion.
Laid back, indulgent.
And according to critics
Yanks in particular
an excuse for lowered expectations
an ideology for the irresponsible.

Who cared about critics?
She'll Be Right seemed right to him.
The Kiwi attitude condensed from
the Polynesian prototype he encountered
in the grass-roofed bungalow in Pago Pago
where for six days running
his seven a.m. wake-up
arrived with artless good cheer
at quarter-to-nine.
He complained on the first day.
On the fourth he converted.

Salutary wisdom from a cabbie
(he made the plane on time)
on the streets of Auckland
(with more Polynesians than any city in the world).
He was ready to listen.

In his new realm of relaxed criteria
old inhibitions were loosened.
Despite Delphic advice from his boss
on the virtues of moderation
he decided to pursue the Coromandel girl
(with the Cook Islands boyfriend)
who backed her bottom into his crotch
in the undersized elevator at work.

He thought, *Why not?*
He thought, *What the hell?*
He told himself, *She'll Be Right!*

It was good to be back in Boston, but
he would like to have lingered Down Under
longer than they let him.

Switchback

from the turn in the switchback a paw
disappeared into the bushes below Rainbow Falls
like the frowning face-rocks guarding the arroyo
your expression seemed to ask why (or why me)

it wasn't a bear of course
though grizzly scat
piled high by the wellspring

the plan was to spend two nights at the climbers' cabin
to look at the arc of our lives
to decide whether once and for all—

your eyeglasses rimed from cataract spray
cheeky chipmunks striped-back squirrels
skittering away from lumbering boots

to have a genuine discussion
a meeting of minds
a really good fight or a really great fuck

later—in darkness—a blue laser-eye
beams across the city—reflects
off the Transamerica pyramid—
lighting up the North Beach apartment
where the phone never rings and
no one is there to answer the question

On the Sundial Bridge

I don't know what's gotten into M
she marches across the glass footbridge
as if she owns it
as if she has been here before
I think I know better

                    refracted sun flickers
from a tour boat riding the Sacramento
rushing from one rail to the other
she waves down to the captain
who seems to wave back

she holds me like a lover
the smell of September in her forearms
neckline sweat salting my tongue—solano winds
I should have known better

beneath the suspension tower
anchored to the shoreline
couples coming near
slip past in opposite directions

she pulls me close
shrouds me in whispers
every word a question
and I too swift to hear
                    too slow to answer

Way After Sappho

just
now
goldsandaled
Dawn

comes
creeping
slowly
across
the
island
in
the
center
of
the
parking lot
in search of
her door keys
having yet again
boosted one too many
at the Downtown
Boosters' ball

Isidor Wright

Isidor Wright came late to the campaign breakfast.
He took the last available seat, an unexpected slot
at the head table, next to Robert Kennedy.
Isidor ate flapjacks fried for the occasion.
Bobby, toying with his special four-minute egg,
said *we must try to do better.*
Isidor caught Bobby reflected in the side-wall mirror
as he and Teddy left the gathering.
Bobby perished in Los Angeles two weeks later.

In the 2003 run-up to the war in Iraq
Isidor Wright stayed home.
He'd been surprised by the October Surprise of 1980,
also surprised by Operation Urgent Fury on Grenada,
surprised again by the carpet bombing of Panama in 1989.
Iraq was no surprise, but after Desert Storm
in the same country twelve years earlier
he wasn't ready for Shock and Awe
and the wretchedness that was sure to follow.

Isidor Wright ran into G. W. Bush one night
drinking near-beer in a West Texas roadhouse.
When W. couldn't pronounce nuclear correctly
Izzy shot him in the temple with an unlicensed handgun.

.

Loma Prieta

1
feet on a footstool
in her big house in Berkeley
she called her counseling
Zen for the Sensible

>   The End's Not the End
>   Fear's Not Your Father

she had a sizeable following
drawn from both sexes
some came for years

>   Don't Lie to Yourself
>   Don't Dwell on Your Blunders

she published her wisdom
in magazines and booklets
plus annual insertions
in the school board pictorial

from a Big Sur society
came thirty thousand dollars
she hadn't requested

>   Love Is Your Body
>   You Already Own the Stars

2
Loma Prieta
collision on the fault line
never tied to its fundament
the Victorian trembles and fractures

a client on a Vespa is crushed
by the Cypress Street Viaduct
the miniature schnauzer goes missing

she stops granting interviews
shortens her work week
joins the roster of the suicide hot line

>   truth is truth
>   beauty beauty
>   when one door closes others will follow

her daughter moves out of the mansion
now up for sale with no serious takers

3
the therapy group gathers
on the S-shaped walkway
in front of the vestibule
on the locked door a message

>   life is a vessel
>   that will sail out to sea
>   and sink

Birth of the Blues

The sax man's keening note
rising above rooftops
rockets across the world—

You hum to yourself
pinned down by howitzers
next to an ammo dump
three hundred yards from the nearest protection.

from a whippoorwill
out on a hill
they took a new note

Lying prone in the open could be unhealthy.
You missed the lieutenant's talk
on "Hiding from the Enemy"
(And last week's lecture: "Why Are We Here?")

You know how to hide
(when there's time to take cover).
You know why we're here
(and you've never believed it).
You remember the millions who died, went missing
        shelled bombed tortured
        demoralized dishonored
        displaced obliterated
with still more to come, you are the target.

pushed it through a horn
'til it was worn
into a blue note

But things will change—if you make it to the bunker
you rotate tomorrow—if you make it to the bunker.

The truce—signed at 10 this morning—
goes into effect at 10 tonight.
Batteries north and south
using these twelve hours to fire
uncrated explosives at each other
across the 38th parallel.

they nursed it
rehearsed it
and gave out the news. . . .

Shipping News

An American troop ship
on the blustering Pacific
moving four-thousand soldiers
in a non-Navy transport
meant for twenty-one hundred
known widely for its galley
serving denatured powdered eggs
chipped beeflets in a military cream sauce
on oxidized mess gear coated with soap film
washed down with reconstituted orangeade
while inhaling diesel-brown exhaust fumes
containing forty toxic ingredients
excreted from engines of a pre-war maker
that induced headache nausea and confusion
and in my case a great misery in the G.I. department
and a loss of fourteen pounds in the eight days it took
to reach the U.S. repo-depot in Sasebo Japan
en route to taking part in a UN police action
for the Republic of Korea against what
we were told by a light colonel
was a ferocious coalition of North Korean and
Chinese forces that would attack California unless
it was crushed right there in Asia.

It wasn't.

Weekend Pass

Newark's an ice field
LaGuardia's grounded
no trains to Boston till late in the morning

twice delayed the 10:11 crawls through Connecticut
hitting South Station at last in the frost-bit twilight

●

He put on civvies in Norman Oklahoma—
freed early from the army—on the GI Bill—
in an all-white dorm
nine-tenths filled by oilmen of the future
including Frederick T. Farmer
who begged him to enroll in summer session
using Fred's name and ID at Texas A & M
expenses pre-paid plus a thousand in cash
for anything better than a grade of B minus

after Korea—
beer for breakfast
Bed Check Charlie
honey wagons and kimchi—
Oklahoma seemed tolerable
until it wasn't
though he had the stacks to himself
and J. Swift in the library
children of the brain
on those Saturdays the Sooners
were crushing opponents
at the student-packed stadium
led by the all-American tackle
who got a standing O
when the poli-sci prof
singled him out in Government I
on the first day of class

●

Leaving the terminal he hails a taxi
slips on the ice
gashing his eye on the door of the cab—
the terrified driver speeds him fare-free
to Mass. Eye and Ear for thirteen stitches—
he calls his sweetheart but cannot make contact—
she's on skis in Vermont with a draft-deferred friend

he catches the early express
but fails to reach base before the bugler
landing him on the fuckup squad
feeding coal into Fort Dix furnaces
at half-past the hour from midnight to dawn

●

Three days under sombrous skies
and on the fourth
emerging as the clouds decompose
a come-and-go blueness
slowly gaining substance
to materialize finally
prodigiously
as Mt. Rainier—
close
so close
it fills up the world—
he had seen mountains on the long trip west
as his troop train smoked through the Rockies
but caught in kitty-whist combat
two dollars a rubber
his attention ran fickle
and his story holds only the Blue Hills of Milton
half-a-day's hike from trailhead to summit

●

The military transport slips by degrees
through the cedary green of the San Juan Islands—
glints of Oriental amethyst
flashing off the face of Rainier
looking west over the Pacific
to the chaos he knows is waiting

He Didn't Come

yesterday you returned the novella I loaned you
p. 96, bookmarked underlined checked in the margin
he didn't come
a message to me? to yourself?

he didn't come
not that reception all those years ago?
I know you were disappointed
something must have happened
when I said I'd be there I'm sure I meant it

he didn't come
we're not talking sex are we?
not that one time
when you thought it was your fault
and I said of course it wasn't
(of course it wasn't)
the entire sentence reads
Although he promised, he didn't come

he didn't come
is it the promising?
whatever I promised I never pledged
I'm the one in tenuous light
you're the one with percipient eyes
you experience your destiny
I am caught in my past
and if I didn't come

it's because I couldn't
(or didn't think I could)
though now as I reread those words
I believe I might have

In my dream thoughts

I see all four of me
Laugher, weeper, good guy, prick
Laugher's my loved one, whom I would pick to
Nurture my spirit, to lift up my psyche.

Part of me goes for the *prick*
The conscienceless one featured
In fiction, a creature who
Makes his own rules, who knows every trick.

But the sadness that summons the *weeper*
Haunts my days like some limitless curse
Meant to entomb me or worse
To bury the *good guy* still deeper.

Kidneys

My nephrologist says it's our job, hers and mine,
to see that my kidneys outlive me.
She tells me I am suffering from kidney failure.
Not *renal insufficiency*, not *kidney dysfunction*
no: kidney fucking *failure*
a definitive diagnosis, incipient thanatosis.

Wait, calm yourself.
It's failure*s*—in the plural—
slow to develop, appearing in stages.
Stage one: kidneys healthy, productive, sluicing along.
Stage five: kidneys kaput, no longer operational.
Stages two, three and four:
clinical signposts on the pathway to failure.
Our task is to get me to the finish ahead of my kidneys.

My nephrologist reassures me
though my kidneys have long been stage three
(with tinctures of protein in their languishing output)
they're not half bad for someone my age.
I've peed a little protein myself, she says.
Her prescription? *Cut down on bananas.*

At the end will my kidneys look back with love?
Will they wonder whether it's worth it—
straining away in those final few moments—
bereft of affection from my unfeeling heart?

The Watsu Water Massage

I slip into the warmth
a wanderer and his lady
skin on skin
venetian sun slits
continents in motion
the universe ringing

the inside eye
beyond the horizon
the passion fruit island
hot wind in the water
splashed skin in the sunset
rivulets clinging

cradled and precious
I'm three again
her breast
my chest
fish-dive genitalia
a korimako singing

she bows *Namaste*
towels off with a hot springs t-shirt
I put on my glasses
wait for my world to spin to a stop

Norman Jacobson

I missed your memorial
but I had an excuse
I didn't know you were dead.

How could you be dead?
Of our starlit mentors
you were the nonesuch.
Though the catalog said American Political Theory
the nature of genius is what you were after:
Kepler and Madison, Mozart and Edison
Oppenheim DiMaggio Henry Thoreau.

Does eclectic cover it?
Crosscutting disciplines to ponder every new paradox.
James B. Conant: *The hits in science are made*
by crooked balls.
Albert Einstein: *I want to think God's thoughts.*
The rest I leave to the hewers of wood and the carriers of water.

Born in the Bronx.
Schooled in the garment trade.
America through an old bubbe's eyes.
Mournfully smart, generous of heart.
In the Eisenhower brownout
you switched on the lights.

Awakening

At the Needham nursing home
the smell of old people's piss
drifts down to Reception.
Awakening in her room, my mother smiles unclearly
I don't know who you are, she says
but I know I love you.

Apart from the pearl-black Pontiac
rented from Alamo by my older sister
no one notices the six-car cortege
inching along the icy expressway.
The mourners, little more than a minyan,
assemble in the snow around the gravesite—
from a leafless sycamore a crow
stares silently down at the gathering.

Eyes running in the cold the rabbi chants in Hebrew
a prayer carried away by the wind—he asks me,
eldest son, to drop the first spade of earth onto the coffin.

And did you know me when you knew me,
your blue-eyed boy?

The crow, frozen to his tree,
watches the backhoe fill up the ditch
listens to a cawing somewhere in the distance
wonders who in the world could be calling his name.

Ice

In the dog days of August
Her mind is on winter.
Everything under snow.
The chickens in their coops.
Ice thickened beneath her skates.
Laced tight polished white.
In the sunlight of course
But even at night.
At Wagner's Pond.
Streaking away from the marshmallow fire
In the rocks on the shoreline.
Skating backwards with momentum.
Her blades almost noiseless.
The fire diminishing in the dark.
Hips rolling to increase her speed.
Not knowing nor wanting to
What might be behind her.
The free-wheeling of it.
The ice-windiness of it.
The aloneness of it.
And only the one misadventure.
The simple displacement,

Which the neurologist says
Will have to be dealt with.

The smiling weather woman reports
Temperatures hovering at 100
For the fifth day running.

The Lobsterman

downeast dialect
irregular nouns
syntax salted with reticence

guy-wire strength
sun-steeled hair
up-anchored off the dock
at Frenchman Bay

stone-cloud sky by Bigelow Bight
(don't mind a little blowin, he said)
sea scud wicked out east past Penobscot
(lobsterin's lobsterin, he said)

when the nor'easter hit
(said t'wasn't near
calamitous as a
pisshole in a snow bank)

at the memorial they spoke of
sea cocks and grab rails
inboards out of order
Rittenhouse Straight on the rocks

the slate-gray woman in black
you'll never catch me down there, she said
you'll never

Seeing/Unseen

pearly gray the fogbank hovers on the shoreline
the sand sepia
the sea quiescent
the air barely breathing

a faint moon rising over Neahkahnie Mountain

her back to him
she stares through smoke-gray glasses
first at the floorboards
then at the compass pointing steadily south

a drowsy cormorant hunched
on the riprap next to the jetty
two crab-floats motionless on the blackening water
the ebbing sea-voice *rallentando*

a cutthroat splashes
as the outboard turns into the slip
in the semi-dark she trips stepping onto the dock
just catching the pier post (before he can reach her)
and pulls herself safely away from the boat

from the Edgewater Tavern *Happy Hour*
reflects inconstantly on the riverside surface

and you can't seem to see how I crave your affection

Why Didn't You Call?

I waited for you outside the theater.
They were showing *The Long Goodbye*
with Elliott Gould as Philip Marlowe
the one where he serves pet food his cat hates
in the can of the brand she loves
but not to be fooled
she turns up her nose and
skitters out of his life forever
leaving him catless in L.A.
like shitless in January
which is how scared I was
when you were driving home from
your weekend retreat
a scatterbrained friend at the wheel
of a retrograde Fiat
on the snakiest stretch of the Coast Highway
with gusts up to fifty.
before 9/11
before Sarkozy
before Lady Gaga
but not before I knew
I couldn't go on living without you.

P.S. Do You Read Me?

push-pulls and ovals
push-pulls and ovals
pen-in-hand practice the Palmer technique
sweeping stylish disciplined well-mannered
an alphabet leaning softly right

followed by a revolution in pencraft
Palmer out Rhinehart in
push-pulls abandoned
characters sturdy ascenders at attention
vertical rational quick

followed by a feminine readjustment
post-Palmer girls dotted i's with circles
crossed t's with tildes
pinned a pig's tail on the ends of agreeable consonants

your own hand held steady over the decades
I have your note from two years ago
written at forty in middle school cursive
lowercase letters with outstretched extenders
as if reaching to caress the characters that follow

in a feverish scribble I penciled back a message
did you get it?
could you read it?
did you run out of stamps?

Anomie

1
to make way for a future freeway
the once-grand houses are condemned
purchased and rented to grad students with children;
one by one the buildings are leveled and
as the houses vanish
the children
    grow disobedient
    travel in packs
    speak their own language
    stay out all night

2
at the survey research center
I work on a study of anomie
or is it alienation
I can't tell the difference

3
I live in a big house
call it a fortress
box-beamed ceilings
walls of concrete
set deep in bedrock
to last forever

4
on a class trip to Texas
someone's son—call him Jim—
persuades a pal with a cell phone
to text Jim's girlfriend at school
that Jimmy's been shot dead in the street
the girl runs to the principal
who informs Jim's father

5
the survey research center is now
a medical complex specializing
in disorders of the mind
including one discovered in their own clinic
they call it Transcendental Dislocation

6
the big house is empty
the roof may be leaking
no one knows
where Jimmy went

Whose Woods

Shirley Weneski sole survivor of those
gathered in the gazebo to get out of the torrent
stated she didn't realize it was a dope party
she'd been walking in the woods all day
attracted to the garden by the boom box
and they all joined in on *Factory Girl*
one of her special faves when Mick sings
she ain't come out yet and she didn't know
any of the victims except
this guy playing guitar was named Star
and his girlfriend was Mingy
short for Virginia

there were too many footprints in all directions
the festival the night before
catered by the marijuana super store
earned the city $9,000 in sales tax
which paid for extra police on overtime
but when the storm hit the cops ran for cover
and no one saw who planted the IED in the mulberry

a little-known group the Fraternal Iago Brothers
(FIB) claimed credit in ten tweets
its leader said she had zero against the festival per se
but why did they go ahead and hold it
after she told them it was the very night FIB scheduled
its annual hazing of new members at a nearby secret location
I am not a teacher
I am an awakener

Speaking to the Police Department Ladies Auxiliary
Chief Bud Doble said they hadn't ruled out terrorism
but given the homemade nature of the explosives
the suspects could be local loonies on meth

it won't be easy he said *but we'll get those fuckers*
you'll pardon my French
a spokesperson from NSA said they had nothing
definite on FIB even though they had rapidly
reexamined three point five million phone calls
made in the previous six months within a ten-mile radius
and put thirty additional assets on the case
we're not out of the woods on this one she said

your narrator knows Shirley from another poem
about her brother who served overseas
but was discharged dishonorably
for refusing a fourth rotation to the Middle East
where he was twice wounded
OD-ing thirteen times on addictive pain killers
the narrator is also aware that Shirley had not been
alone in the woods before she appeared at the party

he will not finger her because why the hell should he
though that valley girl gabble ought to be a felony

Rainy Day Rumblings

My wife's been writing poems about water and
this poem was going to be about water too
but it's been raining cats and dogs
shorthairs and shih tzus
pronounced shit-soos by my brother in Texas,
the underfoot kind that like to romp in the rain
unlike my brother who's nevertheless often
wet, as in all, and also dry, as in boring,
as in the tunneling proposed to shoot trains from
Market Street to Fisherman's Wharf
even though the fishermen long ago sailed up-coast
to Bodega Bay and beyond
leaving in their wake Believe It or Not!
cracked crab on the sidewalks
and *trattorias anginas*
not that my brother gives a *fico* about the Bay Area
which he visits only rarely
on his way to Osaka say
or as an extension of a gambling trip kept secret
from his only wife who
if she knew he was burning Benjamins in Vegas
wouldn't think twice about leaving him
out in the rain.

If she asked me would I tell her?
As one herring said to the other
am I my brother's kipper?

David Carlson's *Quantum Quartet*

we need no violins—
the viola—reassuring resonance—
consoling baritone—
and one protracted high note
fading like the half-heard call of a vanishing bird

clarinet silk through the upper registers—
flute-like tremolo warily descending—
(please save yourself—us—
it's not yet too late)

in the middle "*desolato*"
an interlude on tape—
picked up, prolonged by breathing musicians—
istesso tempo to an unstable silence

then the finale—"*allegro energico*"—
forty fingers blurred in motion—
wave after wave—pulsing, *prestissimo*—
(how much is—how many are there—left to be lost?)
wave upon wave—*con agitazione*—

and at the crucial moment a clarinet cadenza—
seizing us—arcing us far beyond memory—
into the night with no thought of safety

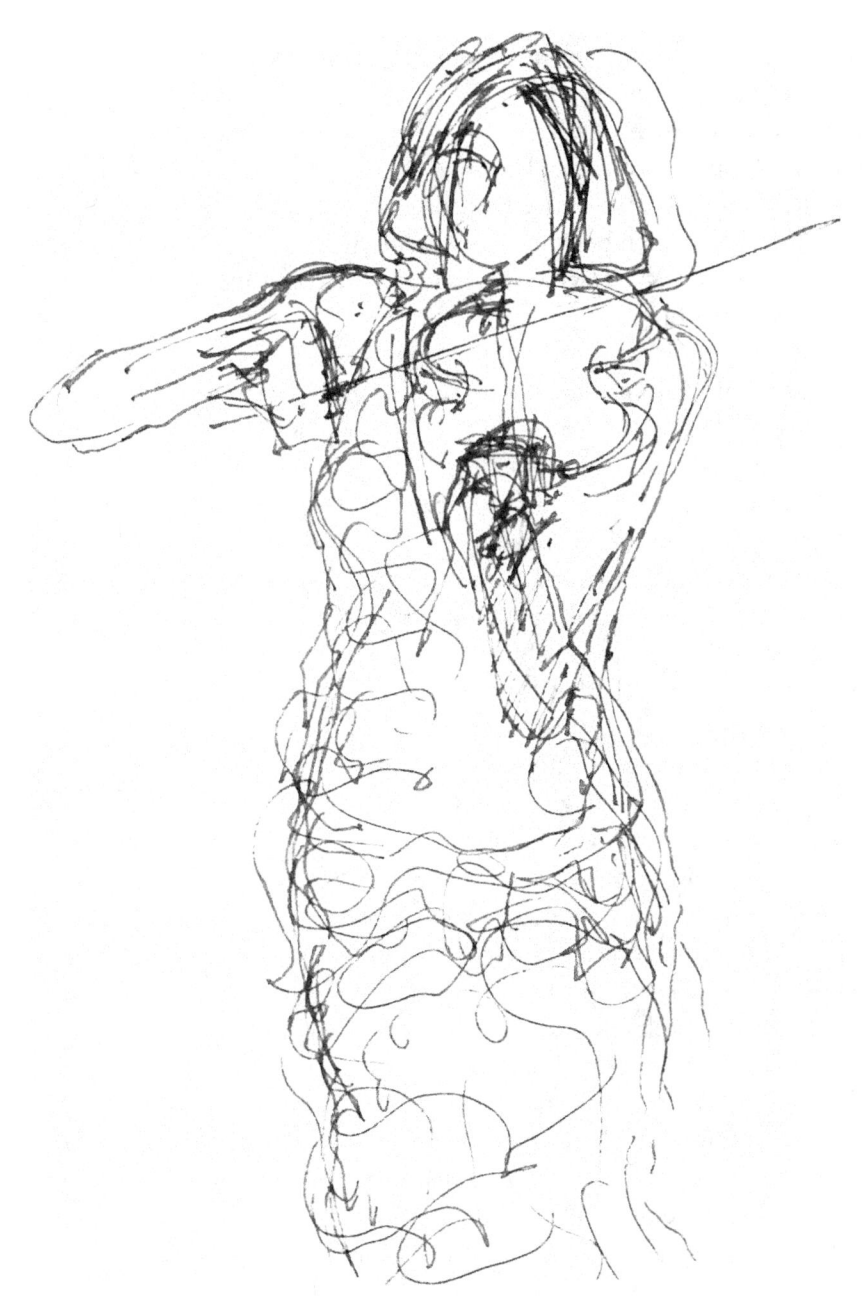

ALL

it was *Bondi's* Pharmacy where we filled our prescriptions
at least I think it was Bondi's
I'm sure it started with a B
but yes it could have been a D
on the I.V. bag D stands for Decadron
even if I don't remember the store's first letter
I definitely know the town it was in and it wasn't Stoughton
we hated Stoughton
I'm not certain why we hated it
any more for example than we hated Holbrook or Attleboro
they were all tasteless weren't they
and Stoughton had a square
we had to settle for Washington Street
(no it wasn't Main for god's sake)
which was called something else
where it began by the public golf links
meandered through the six-block business section
which included Jack's Men's Shop
where I was let go after three months
when Jack realized that a high school jock
would not bring in teenage customers
then with yet another street name
came to an end five miles later
at the Four Corners near the Hospital School
they're pumping Decadron into me
which at once elevates my blood sugars
and floods me with energy
so I can talk non-stop for hours about stuff
I've got it ALL here (get it?)
Acute Lymphoblastic Leukemia
which features a severe shortage of platelets
a word I once thought meant dishes
falling between dinner-sized and sandwich
Dedham Street runs off Washington

with the historical society on the northwest corner
(don't imagine the Ded in Dedham derives from death
the street is so called because it leads to Dedham
a town named after the rustic village
 in Colchester Essex where John Constable
who died suddenly in 1837 from undetermined causes
did a painting of the mill owned by his father)
it will take you to the Blue Hills Country Club
the town's private golf course
(which once hosted a professional tournament)
where I was fired for refusing to tote a member's bag
when the caddy-master reneged on his promise
to let me play a half-round after I had carried doubles
for 18 holes in 95° heat in the morning
this afternoon I'll hear the findings of the Philadelphia
Chromosome Test that will indicate
whether or not I will need a bone-marrow transplant
I am/will be interested
in getting
the result
later

Goodbye

Help me look without crying—Jaime Sabine
                translated by Sam Drukman

The old Silver Bridge
spanning the Big Hole River outside Divide
Pumphouse Road to Powerhouse Fishing Site
has been closed
temporarily they say

A gusset plate that bound the trusses
has gone decrepit and
so has the superstructure
battered by vehicles
for more than a century

Thirty miles to the east and
forty minutes from Butte
Sam sits waiting
in the straw-bale house
he put up himself

On his Kindle he plays Scrabble
four games at a time
once a master
now entranced by board symmetry
in ten minutes he's tired
exhausted in twenty

Say goodbye to the old Silver Bridge
to remove it a hundred thousand dollars
to fix it a million
say goodbye goodbye
say goodbye

Contingent breath from the silence of the bedroom
thoughts tapering in Sam's Harbor of Dreams
already he sees the abandoned island
steelhead gold in the dying sun

. . . for Sore Eyes

I'm twenty-three.
My parents and brothers and sisters are with me.
We're talking about something that could be important.
But they're speaking in slo-mo diphthongs and
Everyone's dispersing.
Where are they going?

I spent most of that summer at the family flat
on Spencer Street listening to Art Mooney
Sarah Vaughn Lily Pons Teresa Brewer
and the Red Sox
cared for by my sweetheart kid sister
my eyes bandaged
recovering from a third strabismal surgery
during which I was kept awake
on the operating table answering questions
in a wilderness of cocaine and opium

I don't recognize this place with its stadium-sized hallway.
No editorial staff.
No classrooms.
No office for me.
No one who knows who I am.
I can't stay here.

Siblings are gone.
It's just me and my mother and my father.
The deadliest dead-end.
And some woman who insists I do
something I don't want to.
I'm young.
Somewhere else.
With someone else.

my sister said I should continue
convalescing at home
but I had to get out
I was twenty-three

at Mindy's poolroom
bandages off
I shoot nineball from ten to eight
in the phlegmatic murk of six-inch coronas

I lumber back to the flat
clothes clothed in cigar smoke
fingers coated a chalk-dust blue
an old man's eyes burnt and burning

my sister's not there

Still Life

It wasn't that I couldn't see you
>in your Oldsmobile repos rust-blue Torinos
>cannibalized Caddies batteries discharging

God knows I could see you
>bondoed Impalas oxidized Fieros
>unlicensed Le Barons upholstery in the windows

It's that I never reached you
>junk in your driveway junk in your veins
>exhaust in the house you no longer owned

And you didn't want to reach me
>I don't give a shit, you said
>I'm as good as anyone, you said
>punch a face when I feel like
>and nobody's time clock
>crack a cold one for breakfast
>work the needle at night

>I *know* what I'm doing, you said

At the same time you knew
beneath all the bombast
that jumper cables couldn't stretch
to the heart's-ease you longed for

Alone on the margins of life
    the cops were a menace
        the landlord a bastard
            the car was impounded
                the ex fell to pieces
                    the body corroded
                        the mind lost its bearings

The mind lost its bearings
One wheel kept spinning
Then stopped

The Grief Group

Like light, Grief strikes us in waves.
Invisible, odorless, except when she isn't—and artful—
a dead ringer for panic, hesitation, annoyance.
Can't decide? Off your feed? Feeling pissed?
Grief has overcome you.

Or hasn't.
Grief makes a note in her log book.

At the treatment center clinicians are in doubt.
Lawrence felt depressed and anxious
long before his traumatic episode.
Do his current symptoms rise from PTSD
or from his earlier neuroses?
Grief likes these kinds of questions.

Grief leads us up the stairs to our familiar meeting room.
Our group: six women, two men.
Among our dead are:
  two husbands
  two sons
  one mother
  one father
  one brother
  one long-term lover

Millie can't focus on fixing her house.
The roof. The rugs.
The downstairs plumbing.
Grief asks, what's all this to do with me?

Sandy's having trouble at the co-op.
Nobody likes her.
And now her canary has died.
Your *canary*, says Grief, give me a break.

Billie can't keep her finances straight.
Her husband paid the bills. The taxes.
Dealt with the lawyers.
That isn't grief, Grief shouts, that's lost co-dependence.

I present a dream in which I'm buried in a fog bank.
I grope my way out
but the sun is so bright it gives me a headache.
Grief asks, what did you have for supper?

Grief wishes to be clear:
do not, she says, confuse everyday angst with what I'm about.
Despite appearances, Grief is a loving instructor.
She knows she's the pain that afflicts us,
precursor to most of our tears.
She wants only comprehension of who she is
and what she wishes to accomplish.

If we let her
Grief would teach us to live on without her.
Her deepest desire is to leave us alone.

A Conversation

his words
pleases/howevers/be-reasonables—
shoot speedily through her mind
weightless unregistered

he tells her his head hurts
the aura the pressure far beyond thresholds
a migraine with a headache

she cannot listen
four in the morning bottle long emptied
her doctor be damned

he says let me put it this way
meaning why won't you listen
she says what do you mean
he points to his headache
she says I can't hear you

•

in the pre-dawn black
the silence is carnage

Mechanical Disadvantage

1
Bubbe treadaling her Singer.
Whick-whick-a-whick rising/dropping.
Cotton stitches stitching cotton.
The floor lamp in dark suffusion.

2
Outside, his screams peal past Rosenbaum's barn.
Thirteen C-hooked sutures pulled tight
to close the wound in a jagged crescent.
 (Family doc forgot his Novocain.)

3
I said put your backs into it boys
to sound as if I were in charge
as if I'd measured twice.
No, that's not right.

What I said was I'm certain there's
an advantage travelling the distance
over which effort is applied
if you can do so without friction.

4
There is light at the end of your tunnel
if you can slip quick through the darkness.
A screw is an inclined plane wrapped around a cylinder.
A scream can last a lifetime.

5
Uncoupled
    My mind has hit a nerve.
    My nights run on to endless.
    The chasms in my dreams are laced with arrows.
    My vanishing point has disappeared
                      but still I see it coming.

Getting in Touch

I hadn't heard from myself in weeks
and had begun to wonder
were there fragmentary bulletins
hidden behind file drawers
secrets too risky to let myself in on

not that I couldn't get through the days
headlights on thermostat down
molars flossed crosswords finished
feverfew saw palmetto
fortnights vanishing at the speed of life

I even managed to *accomplish things*
license renewed gaskets replaced
dry rot retarded will reexamined
will re-reexamined

resonant decrees: *on termination*
of course unmistakable silence decoded
earphones snugged volume on high

in perpetuity—not *your* duration
testamentary hopes for somebody else
valedictory stipulations:
    irrevocable trust [could be talking love here]
    trust for the truster no questions asked
    sleepwalking over

Once My Moon

that year winter came in August
leaving the peonies dead in their beds
the moon in hiding for ninety-three days

oh moon oh moon oh moon

Van Allen glissandos slipping to earth
coating the forests in icy lament

cry moon oh moon my moon

slumbering oceans tidewater indolence
midnight hangs on the shoreline

oh moon oh moon sweet moon

over the houses a golden illusion
spectral penumbras dissonant harmonics

oh moon dear moon soft moon

on the ninety-fourth day the moon took flight
spiraling off to a faraway galaxy

oh moon oh moon
o once my moon

Note

p. 16: Part of the largest Superfund clean-up site in the country, the 900-foot-deep, one-mile-by-fifteen-mile Berkeley Pit began as a mining operation of the Anaconda Copper Company in the 1950s on the east side of Butte, Montana. Today the open pit is filled with water containing heavy metals, toxic chemicals, and new species of fungi and bacteria. Because of its hugely valuable mineral content, the area was once known as The World's Richest Hill.

Acknowledgements

It has been a great pleasure collaborating with Lisa Esherick, gifted artist, Berkeley neighbor, and a warm friend.

Several of the poems in this book have, at various stages of completion, benefited from the insights of fellow-poets, who (along with me) make up the membership of CLAMB—
Chana Bloch
Lorrie Goldensohn
Anne Barrows
Mason Drukman
Barry Goldensohn
—an intermittent, floating poetry workshop that has met bi-weekly roughly every other year over the past decade, whenever the Goldensohns have been in Berkeley for a sizeable period of time. Thanks to the CLAMBarians for their generous criticism. Thanks also to my good friends Leonard Cottrell and the late Howard Waskow, whose comments and encouragement were exceedingly helpful. My greatest appreciation goes to my wife, Anne Barrows, my first reader, my inspiration, and the love of my life..

Working with Fomite's Marc Estrin and Donna Bister, publishers blessed with great patience and good humor, has been a rewarding and fruitful experience.

About the Author

Born in Boston in 1932, Mason Drukman has had a varied career as factory worker, short-order cook, broadcaster (Armed Forces Radio Service), political scientist (Reed College; University of California, Berkeley), author (*Community and Purpose in America*: McGraw-Hill; *Wayne Morse, A Political Biography*: OHS Press), editor (*The Oregon Times*), administrator (The Learning Community, Portland, Oregon; Consumers Institute, Wellington, New Zealand; Survivors International, San Francisco), and freelance writer: his pieces have appeared in numerous magazines, newspapers and journals. He lives in Berkeley. This is his first book of poetry.

Photo — Don Prichard

About the Artist

Born in San Francisco in 1941 to architect parents, Lisa Esherick studied at the San Francisco Art Institute under Diebenkon, Weeks, Neri, Lobdell and Jefferson. She taught classes at City College of San Francisco from 1976 to 2006, during which time she received an M.F.A. in painting from San Francisco State University. Her work has been exhibited throughout the United States and in Germany, and is held in numerous private and corporate collections. After two decades of making paintings inspired by travels and dealing with people in public places, from train stations and airports to casinos and spas, she has returned to an old love—the cityscape and freeways of San Francisco for her subject. Lately she has been dividing her studio time between painting and making short, stop motion animated films. Lisa maintains her studio in Berkeley. Examples of her work can be seen at lisaesherick.com.

Photo — Don Prichard

Fomite
Burlington, VT

A fomite is a medium capable of transmitting infectious organisms from one individual to another.

"The activity of art is based on the capacity of people to be infected by the feelings of others." Tolstoy, *What Is Art?*

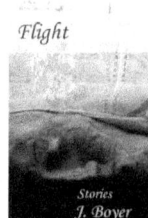

Flight and Other Stories - Jay Boyer
In *Flight and Other Stories,* we're with the fattest woman on earth as she draws her last breaths and her soul ascends toward its final reward. We meet a divorcee who can fly with no more effort than flapping her arms. We follow a middle-aged butler whose love affair with a young woman leads him first to the mysteries of bondage and then to the pleasures of malice. Story by story, we set foot into worlds so strange as to seem all but surreal, yet everything feels familiar, each moment rings true. And that's when we recognize we're in the hands of one of America's truly original talents.

Loisaida - Dan Chodorokoff
Catherine, a young anarchist estranged from her parents and squatting in an abandoned building on New York's Lower East Side, is fighting with her boyfriend and conflicted about her work on an underground newspaper. After learning of a developer's plans to demolish a community garden, Catherine builds an alliance with a group of Puerto Rican community activists. Together they confront the confluence of politics, money, and real estate that rule Manhattan. All the while she learns important lessons from her great-grandmother's life in the Yiddish anarchist movement that flourished on the Lower East Side at the turn of the century. In this coming-of-age story, family saga, and tale of urban politics, Dan Chodorkoff explores the "principle of hope" and examines how memory and imagination inform social change.

Improvisational Arguments - Anna Faktorovich
Improvisational Arguments is written in free verse to capture the essence of modern problems and triumphs. The poems clearly relate short, frequently humorous, and occasionally tragic stories about travels to exotic and unusual places, fantastic realms, abnormal jobs, artistic innovations, political objections, and misadventures with love.

Carts and Other Stories - Zdravka Evtimova
Roots and wings are the key words that best describe the short story collection *Carts and Other Stories,* by Zdravka Evtimova. The book is emotionally multilayered and memorable because of its internal power, vitality and ability to touch both your heart and your mind. Within its pages, the reader discovers new perspectives and true wealth, and learns to see the world with different eyes. The collection lives on the borders of different cultures. *Carts and Other Stories* will take the reader to wild and powerful Bulgarian mountains, to silver rains in Brussels, to German quiet winter streets, and to wind-bitten crags in Afghanistan.
This book lives for those seeking to discover the beauty of the world around them, and will have them appreciating what they have—and perhaps what they have lost as well.

Fomite
Burlington, VT

Zinsky the Obscure - Ilan Mochari
"If your childhood is brutal, your adulthood becomes a daily attempt to recover: a quest for ecstasy and stability in recompense for their early absence." So states the 30-year-old Ariel Zinsky, whose bachelor-like lifestyle belies the torturous youth he is still coming to grips with. As a boy, he struggles with the beatings themselves; as a grownup, he struggles with the world's indifference to them. *Zinsky the Obscure* is his life story, a humorous chronicle of his search for a redemptive ecstasy through sex, an entrepreneurial sports obsession, and finally, the cathartic exercise of writing it all down. Fervently recounting both the comic delights and the frightening horrors of a life in which he feels—always—that he is not like all the rest, Zinsky survives the worst and relishes the best with idiosyncratic style, as his heartbreak turns into self-awareness and his suicidal ideation into self-regard. A vivid evocation of the all-consuming nature of lust and ambition—and the forces that drive them.

Kasper Planet: Comix and Tragix - Peter Schumann
The British call him Punch; the Italians, Pulchinella; the Russians, Petruchka; the Native Americans, Coyote. These are the figures we may know. But every culture that worships authority will breed a Punch-like, anti-authoritarian resister. Yin and yang—it has to happen. The Germans call him Kasper. Truth-telling and serious pranking are dangerous professions when going up against power. Bradley Manning sits naked in solitary; Julian Assange is pursued by Interpol, Obama's Department of Justice, and Amazon.com. But—in contrast to merely human faces—masks and theater can often slip through the bars. Consider our American Kaspers: Charlie Chaplin, Woody Guthrie, Abby Hoffman, the Yes Men—theater people all, utilizing various forms to seed critique. Their profiles and tactics have evolved along with those of their enemies. Who are the bad guys that call forth the Kaspers? Over the last half century, with his Bread & Puppet Theater, Peter Schumann has been tireless in naming them, excoriating them with Kasperdom....*from Marc Estrin's Foreword to Planet Kasper*

The Co-Conspirator's Tale - Ron Jacobs
There's a place where love and mistrust are never at peace; where duplicity and deceit are the universal currency. *The Co-Conspirator's Tale* takes place within this nebulous firmament. There are crimes committed by the police in the name of the law. Excess in the name of revolution. The combination leaves death in its wake and the survivors struggling to find justice in a San Francisco Bay Area noir by the author of the underground classic *The Way the Wind Blew: A History of the Weather Underground* and the novel *Short Order Frame Up*.

All the Sinners Saints - Ron Jacobs
A young draftee named Victor Willard goes AWOL in Germany after an altercation with a commanding officer. Porgy is an African-American GI involved with the international Black Panthers and German radicals. Victor and a female radical named Ana fall in love. They move into Ana's room in a squatted building near the US base in Frankfurt. The international campaign to free Black revolutionary Angela Davis is coming to Frankfurt. Porgy and Ana are key organizers and Victor spends his days and nights selling and smoking hashish, while becoming addicted to heroin. Police and narcotics agents are keeping tabs on them all. Politics, love, and drugs. Truths, lies, and rock and roll. *All the Sinners Saints* is a story of people seeking redemption in a world awash in sin.

Fomite
Burlington, VT

Short Order Frame Up - Ron Jacobs

1975. America as lost its war in Vietnam and Cambodia. Racially tinged riots are tearing the city of Boston apart. The politics and counterculture of the 1960s are disintegrating into nothing more than sex, drugs, and rock and roll. The Boston Red Sox are on one of their improbable runs toward a postseason appearance. In a suburban town in Maryland, a young couple are murdered and another young man is accused. The couple are white and the accused is black. It is up to his friends and family to prove he is innocent. This is a story of suburban ennui, race, murder, and injustice. Religion and politics, liberal lawyers and racist cops. In *Short Order Frame Up*, Ron Jacobs has written a piece of crime fiction that exposes the wound that is US racism. Two cultures existing side by side and across generations--a river very few dare to cross. His characters work and live with and next to each other, often unaware of each other's real life. When the murder occurs, however, those people that care about the man charged must cross that river and meet somewhere in between in order to free him from (what is to them) an obvious miscarriage of justice.

Loosestrife - Greg Delanty

This book is a chronicle of complicity in our modern lives, a witnessing of war and the destruction of our planet. It is also an attempt to adjust the more destructive blueprint myths of our society. Often our cultural memory tells us to keep quiet about the aspects that are most challenging to our ethics, to forget the violations we feel and tremors that keep us distant and numb.

When You Remember Deir Yassin - R. L. Green

When You Remember Deir Yassin is a collection of poems by R. L. Green, an American Jewish writer, on the subject of the occupation and destruction of Palestine. Green comments: "Outspoken Jewish critics of Israeli crimes against humanity have, strangely, been called 'anti-Semitic' as well as the hilariously illogical epithet 'self-hating Jews.' As a Jewish critic of the Israeli government, I have come to accept these accusations as a stamp of approval and a badge of honor, signifying my own fealty to a central element of Jewish identity and ethics: one must be a lover of truth and a friend to the oppressed, and stand with the victims of tyranny, not with the tyrants, despite tribal loyalty or self-advancement. These poems were written as expressions of outrage, and of grief, and to encourage my sisters and brothers of every cultural or national grouping to speak out against injustice, to try to save Palestine, and in so doing, to reclaim for myself my own place as part of the Jewish people." Poems in the original English are accompanied by Arabic translations.

Roadworthy Creature, Roadworthy Craft - Kate Magill

Words fail but the voice struggles on. The culmination of a decade's worth of performance poetry, *Roadworthy Creature, Roadworthy Craft* is Kate Magill's first full-length publication. In lines that are sinewy yet delicate, Magill's poems explore the terrain where idea and action meet, where bodies and words commingle to form a strange new flesh, a breathing text, an "I" that spirals outward from itself.

Fomite
Burlington, VT

Visiting Hours - Jennifer Anne Moses
Visiting Hours, a novel-in-stories, explores the lives of people not normally met on the page -AIDS patients and those who care for them. Set in Baton Rouge, Louisiana, and written with large and frequent dollops of humor, the book is a profound meditation on faith and love in the face of illness and poverty.

The Listener Aspires to the Condition of Music - Barry Goldensohn
"I know of no other selected poems that selects on one theme, but this one does, charting Goldensohn's career-long attraction to music's performance, consolations and its august, thrilling, scary and clownish charms. Does all art aspire to the condition of music as Pater claimed, exhaling in a swoon toward that one class act? Goldensohn is more aware than the late 19th century of the overtones of such breathing: his poems thoroughly round out those overtones in a poet's lifetime of listening."
John Peck, poet, editor, Fellow of the American Academy of Rome

The Derivation of Cowboys & Indians - Joseph D. Reich
The Derivation of Cowboys & Indians represents a profound journey, a breakdown of the American Dream from a social, cultural, historical, and spiritual point of view. Reich examines in concise detail the loss of the collective unconscious, commenting on our contemporary postmodern culture with its self-interested excesses, on where and how things all go wrong, and how social political practice rarely meets its original proclamations and promises. Reich's surreal and self-effacing satire brings this troubling message home. *The Derivation of Cowboys & Indians* is a desperate search and struggle for America's literal, symbolic, and spiritual home.

Views Cost Extra - L.E. Smith
Views that inspire, that calm, or that terrify all come at some cost to the viewer. In *Views Cost Extra* you will find a New Jersey high school preppy who wants to inhabit the "perfect" cowboy movie, a rural mailman disgusted with the residents of his town who wants to live with the penguins, an ailing screen-writer who strikes a deal with Johnny Cash to reverse an old man's failures, an old man who ponders a young man's suicide attempt, a one-armed blind blues singer who wants to reunite with the car that took her arm on the assembly line and more. These stories suggest that we must pay something to live even ordinary lives.

Entanglements - Tony Magistrale
A poet and a painter may employ different mediums to express the same snow-blown afternoon in January, but sometimes they find a way to capture the moment in such a way that their respective visions still manage to stir a reverberation, a connection. In part, that's what *Entanglements* seeks to do. ot so much for the poems and paintings to speak directly to one another, but for them to stir points of similarity.

Fomite
Burlington, VT

Travers' Inferno - L.E. Smith

In the 1970's, churches began to burn in Burlington, Vermont. If it was arson, no one or no reason could be found to blame. This book suggests arson, but makes no claim to historical realism. It claims, instead, to capture the dizzying 70's zeitgeist of aggressive utopian movements, distrust in authority, escapist alternative lifestyles, and a bewildered society of onlookers. In the tradition of John Gardner's *Sunlight Dialogues*, the characters of *Travers' Inferno* are colorful and damaged, sometimes comical, sometimes tragic, looking for meaning through desperate acts. Travers Jones, the protagonist, is grounded in the transcendent philosophy, epilepsy, arson as purification—and mystified by the opposite sex, haunted by an absent father and directed by an uncle with a grudge. He is seduced by a professor's wife and chased by an endearing if ineffective sergeant of police. There are secessionist Quebecois involved in these church burns who are murdering as well as pilfering and burning. There are changing alliances, violent deaths, lovemaking, and a belligerent cat.

The Empty Notebook Interrogates Itself - Susan Thomas

The Empty Notebook began its life as a very literal metaphor for a few weeks of what the poet thought was writer's block, but was really the struggle of an eccentric persona to take over her working life. It won. And for the next three years everything she wrote came to her in the voice of the Empty Notebook, who, as the notebook began to fill itself, became rather opinionated, changed gender, alternately acted as bully and victim, had many bizarre adventures in exotic locales, and developed a somewhat politically incorrect attitude. It then began to steal the voices and forms of other poets and tried to immortalize itself in various poetry reviews. It is now thrilled to collect itself in one slim volume.

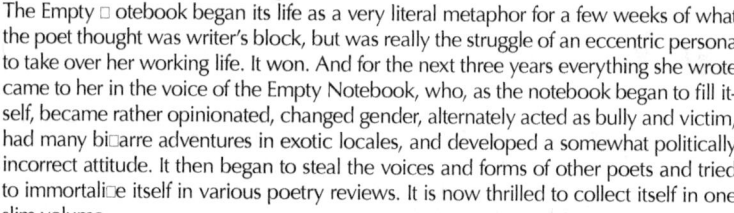
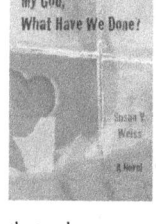

My God, What Have We Done? - Susan Weiss

In a world afflicted with war, toxicity, and hunger, does what we do in our private lives really matter? Fifty years after the creation of the atomic bomb at Los Alamos, newlyweds Pauline and Clifford visit that once-secret city on their honeymoon, compelled by Pauline's fascination with Oppenheimer, the soulful scientist. The two stories emerging from this visit reverberate back and forth between the loneliness of a new mother at home in Boston and the isolation of an entire community dedicated to the development of the bomb. While Pauline struggles with unforeseen challenges of family life, Oppenheimer and his crew reckon with forces beyond all imagining. Finally the years of frantic research on the bomb culminate in a stunning test explosion that echoes a rupture in the couple's marriage. Against the backdrop of a civilization that's out of control, Pauline begins to understand the complex, potentially explosive physics of personal relationships. At once funny and dead serious, *My God, What Have We Done?* sifts through the ruins left by the bomb in search of a more worthy human achievement.

Suite for Three Voices - Derek Furr

Suite for Three Voices is a dance of prose genres, teeming with intense human life in all its humor and sorrow. A son uncovers the horrors of his father's wartime experience, a hitchhiker in a muumuu guards a mysterious parcel, a young man foresees his brother's brush with death on September 11. A Victorian poetess encounters space aliens and digital archives, a runner hears the voice of a dead friend in the song of an indigo bunting, a teacher seeks wisdom from his students' errors and Neil Young. By frozen waterfalls and neglected graveyards, along highways at noon and rivers at dusk, in the sound of bluegrass, Beethoven, and Emily Dickinson, the essays and fiction in this collection offer moments of vision.

Fomite
Burlington, VT

As It Is On Earth - Peter M. Wheelwright
Four centuries after the Reformation Pilgrims sailed up the down-flowing watersheds of ▢ew England, Taylor Thatcher, irreverent scion of a fallen family of Maine Puritans, is still caught in the turbulence. In his errant attempts to escape from history, the young college professor is further unsettled by his growing attraction to Israeli student Miryam Bluehm as he is swept by Time through the "family thing"▢ from the tangled genetic and religious history of his ▢ew England parents to the redemptive birthday secret of Esther Fleur ▢oire Bishop, the Cajun-Passamaquoddy woman who raised him and his younger half-cousin▢ half-brother, Bingham.The landscapes, rivers, and tidal estuaries of Old ▢ew England and the Mayan Yucatan are also casualties of history in Thatcher's story of Deep Time and re-discovery of family on Columbus Day at a high-stakes gambling casino, rising in resurrection over the starlit bones of a once-vanquished Pequot Indian tribe.

Love's Labours - Jack Pulaski
In the four stories and two novellas that comprise *Love's Labors* the protagonists, Ben and Laura, discover in their fervid romance and long marriage their interlocking fates, and the histories that preceded their births. They also learned something of the paradox between love and all the things it brings to its beneficiaries: bliss, disaster, duty, tragedy, comedy, the grotesque, and tenderness. Ben and Laura's story is also the particularly American tale of immigration to a new world. Laura's story begins in Puerto Rico, and Ben's lineage is Russian-Jewish. They meet in City College of ▢ew ▢ork, a place at least analogous to a melting pot. Laura struggles to rescue her brother from gang life and heroin. She is mother to her younger sister▢ their mother Consuelo is the financial mainstay of the family and consumed by work. Despite filial obligations, Laura aspires to be a serious painter. Ben writes, cares for, and is caught up in the misadventures and surreal stories of his younger schi▢ophrenic brother. Laura is also a story teller as powerful and enchanting as Schehera▢ade. Ben struggles to survive such riches, and he and Laura endure.

Signed Confessions - Tom Walker
Guilt and a desperate need to repent drive the antiheroes in Tom Walker's dark (and often darkly funny) stories: a gullible journalist falls for the ▢0-year-old stripper he profiles in a magazine, a faithless husband abandons his family and joins a support group for lost souls., a merciless prosecuting attorney grapples with the suicide of his gay son, an aging misanthrope must make amends to five former victims, an egoistic naval hero is haunted by apparitions of his dead wife and a mysterious little girl.The seven tales in *Signed Confessions* measure how far guilty men will go to obtain a forgiveness no one can grant but themselves.

Body of Work - Andrei Guruianu
Throughout thirteen stories, Body of Work chronicles the physical and emotional toll of characters consumed by the all-too-human need for a connection. Their world is achingly common ▢ beauty and regret, obsession and self-doubt, the seductive charm of loneliness. Often fragmented, whimsical, always on the verge of melancholy, the collection is a sepia-toned portrait of nostalgia ▢ each story like an artifact of our impermanence, an embrace of all that we have lost, of all that we might lose and love again someday.

Fomite
Burlington, VT

The Housing Market - Joseph D. Reich

In Joseph Reich's most recent social and cultural, contemporary satire of suburbia entitled, "The Housing market: a comfortable place to jump off the end of the world," the author addresses the absurd, postmodern elements of what it means, or for that matter not, to try and cope and function, and survive and thrive, or live and die in the repetitive and existential, futile and self-destructive, homogenized, monochromatic landscape of a brutal and bland, collective unconscious, which can spiritually result in a gradual wasting away and erosion of the senses or conflict and crisis of a desperate, disproportionate 'situational depression,' triggering and leading the narrator to feel constantly abandoned and stranded, more concretely or proverbially spoken, "the eternal stranger," where when caught between the fight or flight psychological phenomena, naturally repels him and causes him to flee and return without him even knowing it into the wild, while by sudden circumstance and coincidence discovers it surrounds the illusory-like circumference of these selfsame Monopoly board cul-de-sacs and dead ends. Most specifically, what can happen to a solitary, thoughtful, and independent thinker when being stagnated in the triangulation of a cookie-cutter, oppressive culture of a homeowner's association—a memoir all written in critical and didactic, poetic stanzas and passages, and out of desperation, when freedom and control get taken, what he is forced to do in the illusion of 'free will and volition,' something like the derivative art of a smart and ironic and social and cultural satire.

Still Time - Michael Cocchiarale

Still Time is a collection of twenty-five short and shorter stories exploring tensions that arise in a variety of contemporary relationships: a young boy must deal with the wrath of his out-of-work father—a woman runs into a man twenty years after an awkward sexual encounter—a wife, unable to conceive, imagines her own murder, as well as the reaction of her emotionally distant husband—a soon-to-be-tenured English professor tries to come to terms with her husband's shocking return to the religion of his youth—an assembly line worker, married for thirty years, discovers the surprising secret life of his recently hospitalized wife. Whether a few hundred or a few thousand words, these and other stories in the collection depict characters at moments of deep crisis. Some feel powerless, overwhelmed— unable to do much to change the course of their lives. Others rise to the occasion and, for better or for worse, say or do the thing that might transform them for good. Even in stories with the most troubling of endings, there remains the possibility of redemption. For each of the characters, there is still time.

Raven or Crow - Joshua Amses

Marlowe has recently moved back home to Vermont after flunking his first term at a private college in the Midwest, when his sort-of girlfriend, Eleanor, goes missing. The circumstances surrounding Eleanor's disappearance stand to reveal more about Marlowe than he is willing to allow. Rather than report her missing, he resolves to find Eleanor himself. *Raven or Crow* is the story of mistakes rooted in the ambivalence of being young and without direction.

Fomite
Burlington, VT

The Good Muslim of Jackson Heights - Jaysinh Birjépatil
Jackson Heights in this book is a fictional locale with common features assembled from immigrant-friendly neighborhoods around the world where hardworking honest-to-goodness traders from the Indian subcontinent rub shoulders with ruthless entrepreneurs, reclusive antique-dealers, homeless nobodies, merchant-princes, lawyers, doctors, and IT specialists. But as Siraj and Shabnam, urbane newcomers fleeing religious persecution in their homeland, discover, there is no escape from the past. Weaving together the personal and the political. *The Good Muslim of Jackson Heights* is an ambiguous elegy to a utopian ideal set free from all prejudice.

Meanwell - Janice Miller Potter
Meanwell is a twenty-four-poem sequence in which a female servant searches for identity and meaning in the shadow of her mistress, poet Anne Bradstreet. Although Meanwell herself is a fiction, someone like her could easily have existed among Bradstreet's known but unnamed domestic servants. Through Meanwell's eyes, Bradstreet emerges as a human figure during the Great Migration of the 1600s, a period in which the Massachusetts Bay Colony was fraught with physical and political dangers. Through Meanwell, the feelings of women, silenced during the midwife Anne Hutchinson's fiery trial before the Puritan ministers, are finally acknowledged. In effect, the poems are about the making of an American rebel. Through her conflicted conscience, we witness Meanwell's transformation from a powerless English waif to a mythic American who ultimately chooses wilderness over the civilization she has experienced.

Four-Way Stop - Sherry Olson
If *Thank You* were the only prayer, as Meister Eckhart has suggested, it would be enough, and Sherry Olson's poetry, in her second book, *Four-Way Stop*, would be one. Radical attention, deep love, and dedication to kindness illuminate these poems and the stories she tells us, which are drawn from her own life: with family, with friends, and wherever she travels, with strangers □ who to Olson, never are strangers, but kin. Even at the difficult intersections, as in the title poem, *Four-Way Stop*, Olson experiences □ and offers □ hope, showing us how, *completely unsupervised*, people take turns, with *kindness waving each other on*. Olson writes, knowing that (to quote Czeslaw Milosz) *What surrounds us, here and now, is not guaranteed*. To this world, with her poems, Olson brings □ and teaches □ attention, generosity, compassion, and appreciative joy. —Carol Henrikson

Dons of Time - Greg Guma
"Wherever you look…there you are." The next media breakthrough has just happened. They call it Remote Viewing and Tonio Wolfe is at the center of the storm. But the research underway at TELPORT's off-the-books lab is even more radical -- opening a window not only to remote places but completely different times. □ ow unsolved mysteries are colliding with cutting edge science and altered states of consciousness in a world of corporate gangsters, infamous crimes and top-secret experiments. Based on eyewitness accounts, suppressed documents and the lives of world-changers like □ ikola Tesla, Annie Besant and Jack the Ripper, Dons of Time is a speculative adventure, a glimpse of an alternative future and a quantum leap to Gilded Age London at the tipping point of invention, revolution and murder.

Fomite
Burlington, VT

Screwed – Stephen Goldberg
Screwed is a collection of five plays by Stephen Goldberg, who has written over twenty-five produced plays and is co-founder of the Off Center or the Dramatic Arts in Burlington, Vermont.

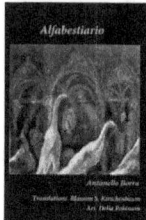 

Alfabestiario
AlphaBetaBestiario - Antonello Borra
Animals have always understood that mankind is not fully at home in the world. Bestiaries, hoping to teach, send out warnings. This one, of course, aims at doing the same.

The Consequence of Gesture - L.E. Smith
On a Monday evening in December of 1980, Mark David Chapman murdered John Lennon outside his apartment building in New York City. The Consequence of Gesture brings the reader along a three-day countdown to mayhem. This book inserts Chapman into the weekend plans of a group of friends sympathetic with his obsession to shatter a cultural icon and determined to perform their own iconoclastic gestures. John Lennon's life is not the only one that hangs in the balance. No one will emerge the same.

Sinfonia Bulgarica – Zdravka Evtimova
Sinfonia Bulgarica is a novel about four women in contemporary Bulgaria: a rich cold-blooded heiress, a masseuse dreaming of peace and quiet that never come, a powerful wife of the most influential man in the country, and a waitress struggling against all odds to win a victory over lies, poverty and humiliation. It is a realistic book of vice and yearning, of truthfulness and schemes, of love and desperation. The heroes are plain-spoken characters, whose action is limited by the contradictions of a society where lowness rules at many levels. The novel draws a picture of life in a country where many people believe that "Money is the most loyal friend of man". Yet the four women have an even more loyal friend: ruthlessness of life.

My Father's Keeper - Andrew Potok
The turmoil, terror and betrayal of their escape from Poland at the start of World War II lead us into this tale of hatred and forgiveness between father and son.

Fomite
Burlington, VT

Unfinished Stories of Girls Catherine ▢obal Dent
The sixteen stories in this debut collection set on the Eastern Shore of Maryland feature powerfully drawn characters with troubles and subjects such as communal guilt over a drunk-driving car accident that kills a young girl, the doomed marriage of a jewelry clerk and an undercover cop, the obsessions of a housecleaner jailed for forging her employers' signatures, the heart-breaking closeness of a family stuck in the snow. Each of Unfinished Stories of Girls' richly textured tales is embedded in the quiet and sometimes violent fields, towns, and riverbeds that are the backdrop for life in tidewater Maryland. Dent's deep love for her region shines through, but so does her melancholic thoughtfulness about its challenges and problems. The reader is invited inside the lives of characters trying to figure out the marshy world around them, when that world leaves much up to the imagination

Writing a review on Amazon, Good Reads, Shelfari, Library Thing or other social media sites for readers will help the progress of independent publishing. To submit a review, go to the book page on any of the sites and follow the links for reviews. Books from independent presses rely on reader to reader communications.

www.ingramcontent.com/pod-product-compliance
Lightning Source LLC
Chambersburg PA
CBHW071213070526
44584CB00019B/3014